Heinz Landon-Burgher

**Putin–Trump–Xi Jinping:
the Tripolar World Order
and the anti-Christian Satanic One-World
Government**

Production and
publishing:
BoD – Books on Demand, Norderstedt
Copyright: 2019 Karl Heinz
Landenberger ISBN 978-3-7526-2480-9

Putin-Trump-Xi Jinping,
the Tripolar World Order
and the anti-Christian Satanic One-World
Government

The End Times

There are ever more signs that point to the fact that we're living in the end times. The satanically unleashed powers of the "deep state" point to the imminent appearance of the Antichrist, who will take over the world.

The Wrath of God

God will put an end to these goings-on in the Last Judgment, and deliver just punishment, namely eternal damnation, to the war criminals with their millions of murders, as well as the criminal politicians, especially in the USA, who have violated human and international rights.

All-forgiving Love

There is a heresy that claims that God understands everything and forgives everything; that, in principle, He forgives all sin, whether the sinners repent and atone for the sin or not. Heinrich Heine mocks: He'd have to forgive me my sins as well — He can't do otherwise. Forgiving is his profession, after all.

Delusion

People who think like this are bound to have their illusions shattered. The suffering, pain, and fear of children tortured by paedophiles, the defilement of women in two world wars and in everyday life, the bombing terrorism on German cities with millions of dead people, including women and children, the drone murders that occur all over the world on a daily basis, the expulsion of entire tribes from their homeland: Silesia, Pomerania, East Prussia, etc., the systematic torture in prison camps, artificially induced famine in Europe, Africa, and the

3

rest of the world, pandemics that are spread deliberately...God is just as outraged by all of this as any normal person would be.

The Russians and the Germans
These two nations, who are very attached to each other and very closely related, suffered and sacrificed more than any other nation during the two world wars.

Russian Revolution
The Russians, in particular, paid a high price with their lives through the Marxist-Communist revolution, which was initiated and financed by the Illuminati and Freemasons and led by Lenin, and had to endure the destruction of more than a thousand years of Russian Orthodox and Czarist history and tradition.

The End of Protestantism
In Germany, parallel to the expulsion of the last German Kaiser, who was highly respected by the people, and the abolition of the Hohenzollern dynasty, the same gang of criminals delivered the fatal blow to Protestantism, whose theology had reached a culminating point.

The Habsburg Empire
The Danube monarchy of the Habsburg Empire, with the Emperor in Vienna, which had already progressed to being a confederation — having overcome the nation state in a humanly legal way — and was in its prime, was also ripped apart against the will of the people. Where Germans and Hungarians fertilised each other culturally and where their capitals vied with each other in their splendour.

Budapest

At first glance, Budapest is almost more impressive than Vienna; the Czechs had their centre in the Golden City of Prague, one of the most beautiful cities in Europe; the Slovaks in Pressburg; the Slovenes and Croats also had wonderful centres in Laibach (Ljubljana) and Zagreb; the Ukrainians and Poles had culturally important centres in Lemberg and Chernivtsi.

The Ottoman Empire

I will come back later to the fragmentation of the Ottoman Empire and the division of the booty, particularly between the British and French, with arbitrary borders drawn between Syria, Iraq and Lebanon, and Palestine and the resulting conflicts that have not been resolved to this day.

Lunacy

The refusal of the Allied powers to enter into a peace treaty with Germany and their continuation of the occupation while maintaining military bases led to increasing conflicts and escalating corruption in the Federal Republic. The lunacy has reached such climaxes in our days that it's becoming clear that things can't go on like this.

Mass Rapes

Mass rapes on New Year's Eve in Cologne, with no convictions — riots at the G20 summit in Hamburg with arson, destruction of buildings, attacks against police officers resulting in very serious injuries — because the perpetrators wear masks, nothing can be established about their identity or charges brought against them.

Antifa

The Green Party in the Bundestag actually want to assist this "Antifa" with financial subsidies. Incidents in Minneapolis, Minnesota, Seattle, that are getting completely out of hand.

Stuttgart

The tranquil city of Stuttgart experienced a "party night" — a "small" group of young people — there are more than 500 who allegedly drank a little too much on this beautiful summer night (a few asylum seekers may have partied too), and then shop windows in Königstrasse were smashed accidentally and shops got looted...a trail of destruction, and the police were powerless. They were no longer in control.

Executive Mayor

Even the Green Executive Mayor, Kuhn, thought that one had to explain to the young people that you don't party like this. He even wished the 19 injured policemen who had to be treated in hospital a speedy recovery. A shining example compared to party members who are of the opinion that the police should be abolished in principle or, as a columnist for taz writes, "dumped into the landfill". Seehofer, Minister of Interior Security, regards this as "an unfortunate phrase".

Kuhn even certified that the policemen's injuries were "not self-inflicted" — which is truly astounding. He means that they did not inflict their injuries on themselves through excessive police violence.

The offer of a peace treaty

The escalating conflicts and revolutionary activity all around the world, the terrorist attacks of all stripes, have led to both Putin and Trump apparently offering to finally end the never-ending succession wars of the Second World War and to resolve all controversial geopolitical issues peacefully through negotiations. Xi Jinping forms part of this league. Our world is to be reorganised under the leadership of the three most powerful men in this world.

Government of unity and consolidation of all institutional powers

Not the one-world government that we're aspiring to, globalisation, i.e. the abolition of all nations and making everyone equal, regardless of their origin, race, skin colour, culture, gender, — and a uniform world religion that everyone has to adhere to and that is created from the union of all religions — Buddhism, Hinduism, Muslims, Judaism and Christianity like the Freemasons want to do.

The Tripolar World Order

The three most powerful men on the globe are presenting the world with a geopolitical variant constituted by this equalisation process.

1. The European landmass stretching from Lisbon to Vladivostok, uniting the multiple European nations under the leadership of Russia, meaning Putin.

2. The richest nation, the USA, together with England and all English-speaking former colonies, i.e. Australia, Canada, New Zealand, etc. under the leadership of Trump.

3. The Pacific region, with the most populous country on earth, which has had an advanced culture for thousands of years, China, together with Japan and all countries with yellow skin are led by Xi Jinping, who connects his mighty empire directly with Central Europe via the new Silk Road.

The Great Hope

The clash of these three statesmen, the most powerful in the world, with the Satanic forces of the Antichrist can be anticipated with much confidence as the hand of the Most High God is obviously over them; and also because these three chosen ones do not employ the criminal means of combat that have been par for the course for the other side for centuries.

Putin

He openly professes Christ. In a marginal situation: the storming of the Dubrovka Theatre in Moscow by 50 armed Chechens and the taking hostage of 850
audience members in order to force Russian troops to retreat from
Chechnya — in this situation, where Putin saw no way of saving the theatregoers, and as the narcotic agent was sprayed into the ventilation system of the building - which did lead to the attackers becoming unconscious and 125 of the theatregoers could no longer be medically revived — in this desperate situation, a direct encounter with Christ obviously took place. This, at least, was what Putin told a journalist.

The Russian Orthodox Church

Accordingly, Putin did everything to bring the Russian Orthodox Church back to life after 70 years of state atheism instituted by the Bolsheviks, and to reinstate a Patriarch that was acknowledged as such by a major part of the population.

The Rebuilding of Churches

Even churches were rebuilt and restored. Much to the chagrin of the US-led Anti-Christ Movement. "Pussy Riots" cast, supported, and financed by US television, is broadcast in all parts of the world. And even Angela Merkel, who is officially the leader of a Christian party, the CDU, felt the need to stand up and reprimand Putin because the performance of godlessness in a Russian cathedral was punished.

First strike

Knowing that Putin is a believer also provides the assurance that he would never strike first in a nuclear war. He also states that quite openly.
However, all warmongers rave about this first-strike doctrine: Bush, Cheney, Rumsfield, Cairns +, Pompeo, Bolton, Hillary

Clinton, Rasmussen, Stoltenberg, etc. Even Uschi van der Leyen would like to reconquer the Crimea peninsula with a nuclear war limited to Europe, and Kramp Karrenbauer wants to scare Putin with a strong NATO armament policy. However, a first strike will most certainly not come from Russia.

Considerations

The American "elite" are deliberating as follows: if we succeed in killing 100 million Russians with a surprise first strike,

the resistance of the survivors will be so weak that at most 4 million on our side will be at risk.

In this way, we'd have the whole Eurasian landmass with its almost inexhaustible supply of raw materials all for ourselves.

A Spoke in the Wheel

The Third World War would have started long ago if Putin hadn't stuck a spoke in the wheel of these strategists; he developed arms and missiles —

at a cost of 64 billion in Russia against 700 billion American defence costs — which fly at such a speed that no US missile defence system can ward them off. Consequently: It will not remain at 4 million deaths, and members of the "elite" could possibly be among those, which has caused these strategists to hesitate.

Pandemics

So, they'd rather focus on pandemics. They were intended to annihilate the 1.5 billion Chinese right from the start anyway. The efficacy of biological weapons was successfully tested for the first time at the end of the First World War. The Spanish flu was a coronavirus, produced in American laboratories and first let loose in the trenches in the Franco-German war zone.

Vaccination

These "Satanists" only ever forget one thing about their crimes: all the soldiers in the trenches were vaccinated, but they forgot to vaccinate their relatives. As the soldiers returned home, they infected their families. Millions died in the USA, England, France, in Germany in any case, and there were 13 million deaths in India. The English like to have people from their colonies fight on their behalf. The estimates are 50–100 million deaths after the end of the war.

Trump

His motto is: "America first". With this, he means that the well-being of the American population is his first priority. Previously, the situation was that the USA waged wars all over the world, in places that the average American had never even heard of, with the aim of conquering oil fields and appropriating mineral resources, the profits of which flow into the coffers of rich entrepreneurs and big banks. The American people, however, never saw this or knew about it, and definitely never got anything out of it.

The Cost of American Military Intervention

Trump reports that the military interventions in the Near East alone cost the country more than 200 billion in the last 10 years. The American economy perished: the "rust belt" where the richest automobile factories once stood; relocation of production to cheaper manufacturing abroad; unemployment, homelessness, illiteracy — 75% of black people in wealthy California cannot read or write.

Trump a Christian

What our press does not reveal: Trump is fighting for a Christian America. The initial ideals of the American state, the ideas of the Pilgrim Fathers, Quakers, Presbyterians, Evangelicals, etc. All those things that are now under siege, he wants to retain as tradition.

Melania, the First Lady, prays the Lord's Prayer with his supporters at his election events. The American press go on a rampage. In Germany, however, they prefer not to mention it, in case it arouses sympathy.

Has our "Christian" Chancellor Merkel ever recited the Lord's Prayer, even once, in her life? To be honest, I can't imagine it. What her father's function in the Christian community was as a clergyman commissioned by the atheist state and paid by Ulbricht, Honecker and comrades, is also a mystery to me.

Assassinations

The CIA is said to have already planned seven assassination attempts on Putin. Although this criminal homicide squad is the most experienced mass murderer in the world, not one of the attempts was successful. All the assassination attempts on Trump also went wrong. Perhaps one can draw the hope from this that both are under the protection of the Most High.

Xi Jinping

A highly likable person, capable, from an honest family — the simplest of backgrounds.

It is a blessing that he can rule for life, and not be exchanged every four years, like the cheap puppets, by those who are not "elected" but who have the "say".

Guidestones

The new world order was established in 1980 with guidelines for the next 1,000 years. In Georgia, they chiselled the guidelines that must be followed for the next 1,000 years of the New World Order into monumental granite. Guidestones can be regarded as stone monuments, comparable to Stonehenge, that provide direction for the coming millennia. The message was chiselled into six granite plates weighing hundreds of tonnes in eight modern languages and four ancient languages: Babylonian cuneiform script,

ancient Greek, Sanskrit and Egyptian hieroglyphs.

The Meaning of the Monument

This monument is so significant that one should download the entire text from the Internet. The financial costs alone are so enormous and the scientific prerequisites for doing all of this in Babylonian, in hieroglyphics, in Sanskrit, etc. that only a tiny number of people are financially able to commission something like this.

Anonymous

The client is apparently an anonymous person. Amazingly, however, this nameless person was carved into the granite with a spelling error. He is called ANONYNOUS. That cannot be a coincidence. It can only mean that the initiated know exactly who this ANON is.

Decalogue

The Decalogue has played a fundamental role in people's lives for the past 3,000 years. They are God's Ten Commandments as Moses received them in the Sinai and carved them on the two stone plates of the Law. This Law for the Chosen People was adopted by the Christians as given by God and the Muslims have also formulated these commandments from God. So, these ten commandments have been valid for all three world religions since 3,000 years ago. The new 10 commandments of the Guidestones are conceived for the next 3,000 years.

The Jewish Commandments

For the "Chosen People", the Israelites, there is no doubt that these commandments were given to them specially by their God, Yahweh. The first sentence makes this clear: "I am the Lord your God...; you shall have no other gods before me".

Details

These commandments refer to the fact that their God brought them out of Egypt into the Promised Land. Apart from the Sabbath rest, the first commandment says: "Honour your father and your mother...".

Fundamental Commandments

The basic instructions for social cohabitation are found in these commandments:

"You shall not murder"

"You shall not steal"

"You shall not commit adultery"

Another Commandment

"You shall not give false testimony". Strictly speaking, these commandments were only meant for the Israelites and their conduct towards one another. The expression "your neighbour" refers only to a member of the same clan, tribe, or one of the twelve tribes descended from Jacob.

Interpreting the Commandments

These commandments were interpreted in the book of Moses already and punishments conceived for violations. When, for example, an Israelite killed a slave, there was no punishment, because he suffered the damage himself and had to buy a new slave. If he killed someone else's slave, he had to replace the value of this slave so that the other person could buy a new slave. If an Israelite killed a non-Israelite, the Decalogue does not provide for any punishment. The laws only relate to the God Yahweh and the Israelites. For example, Moses killed an Egyptian in anger, and was therefore pursued by the Egyptian Pharaoh. For Moses himself this homicide was without importance. The commandment "You shall not steal" also states that you only have to respect the property relations of the tribesmen; this restriction is not imposed towards strangers. As these foreigners may of course defend themselves, an Israelite should definitely be careful when stealing.

The Christian Meaning of the Ten Commandments

As Christians regard the Jewish God of Moses as the same God that Jesus preaches about, the commandments acquired a new meaning. The commandment "You shall not murder" now comprised not only Israelite tribe members, but rather all people. The "neighbour" was now not only from the tribes descended from Jacob, but people in general. Murder and homicide are universal sins.

Extending the interpretation

Extension of the interpretation of theft, robbery and adultery means that they are generally crimes that displease God and are therefore also valid for Christianity as a whole.

The Ten Commandments among Muslims

Mohammed mentions the ten commandments of Moses in the Quran. These ten commandments are fundamental for Muslims as well. They are divided into five commandments and five prohibitions. For Muslims, they are universal and generally applicable right from the start.

Idolatry

In Mohammed's time, the Arabian tribes still worshipped several deities. So that for him, the first commandment is also "You shall not assign companions to him, Allah, i.e. serve no other gods". Accordingly, in the second place there is the commandment "Honour your father and mother: you should

14

show kindness to your parents", i.e. one should also help their parents when they are old and needy because they have raised you as children.

Infanticide

With a totally new commandment that is not found with either Jews or Christians, Mohammed states: "Do not kill your children because of impoverishment". The living conditions of the time were apparently so difficult that parents who could not feed their children killed them. Accordingly, this could apply to abortion today, which women perform because they cannot imagine being able to bring up the child. That does not please Allah.

Orphans

The difficult living conditions also meant that many people died before their children were grown, so that there were many orphans around. Since the orphans were not able not defend themselves yet, many people tried to take away their parents' assets. In contrast, Mohammed required: "Do not approach the assets of orphans."

Full measure and weight

The Arabian tribes traded extensively. They often travelled great distances for months on end with their caravans. In other regions they had different measures and types of weight and money. Mohammed demands "give full measure and weight in accordance with justice." Fair trade should also take place in other countries.

False testimony before the court

"You should not give false testimony in court" was generally understood by the Israelites as not testifying to the jeopardy of members of the tribe, so that they didn't suffer any disadvantage. In contrast, Mohammed says: "If you give testimony in court, be just, including in the case of a relative."

15

Alternative draft

The 10 commandments of the New Age are directly opposed to the biblical Decalogue. Religion, and with it, God, has lost its controlling influence: "God is dead" Nietzsche preaches in the Zarathustra. The Age of Reason has commenced. The French Revolution declares war on God. The Church is the point of attack for the revolutionaries, even more than the monarchy and nobility: Priests are hanged — get the torches! Monasteries are disbanded and all property belonging to the clergy, all churches and other property expropriated.

The Crowning of Reason

In Notre Dame in Paris, human reason is symbolically crowned as the queen of humanity. The Age of Enlightenment, and the enlightened one, the Illuminatus, the leader of the new humanity, is heralded. These enlightened Freemasons are inspired by the "Light-bearer" — Lucifer - who puts an end to the superstition of the religions.

Heralds and hearers

If God himself spoke to his "chosen people" the Israelites in the Old Covenant, now it is the masterminds of the new religion — Voltaire, Rousseau, Marx — who decree their guidelines for the future world government.

Georgia Guidestones

These ten "commandments", guidelines, or directives have been sandblasted into the granite in eight different languages. The very first prescription is already astounding. At the time the guidestones were erected in 1980, the world population had grown to 4 billion; in the meantime, it has doubled to around 8 billion.

The First Commandment
MAINTAIN HUMANITY
UNDER 500 MILLION

Who pronounces this order? And who should carry it out? Who is the authorised representative who issues this order, and who should carry it out? One suspects the future world government.
And how must this instruction be implemented? Must 7.5 billion people be killed, so that only 500 million are left, and in which way should humanity be reduced to this extent?

They thought about a Third World War with nuclear bombs. This notion has lost its persuasiveness among those in control because Russia, the second major nuclear power, now has defence missiles
and attack missiles 10 times the speed of sound that can no longer be intercepted by the Americans, so that the ruling class must now acknowledge that their idea of a first strike can no longer be executed without risk to themselves.
The latest notion is to make all of humanity infertile with one vaccination. They want to start in Africa, but a forced vaccination is also to be ordered in Europe and the USA. This is what the World Health Organisation, under the direction of Bill Gates, aims for. Bill Gates is best friends with Rockefeller, for whom population control is a priority, as he confirms in many speeches.

The Second Commandment
GUIDE REPRODUCTION
WISELY —
IMPROVING FITNESS
AND DIVERSITY

The future world government must direct reproduction and improve optimal genetic material at the same time.

That means that there will be no more fathers and mothers. No more loving couples who can produce children, but procreation should rather be directed by the government, while at the same time striving for breeding ideals and improving DNA through genetic manipulation. Hereditary material is to be selected by the responsible government agencies, i.e. sperm and egg cells will also be selected from there and mixed, crossed, and combined depending on the purpose. The living beings that arise as a result will never know who the male semen or the female egg cell came from.

The Third Commandment
UNITE HUMANITY WITH
A LIVING NEW LANGUAGE

A uniform language spoken by all should be created to replace the diversity of the languages of all peoples. This language should be a new, artificially created language, comparable to Esperanto. In plain language, however, this means that all the human knowledge laid down in languages will be thrown on the garbage heap. The Word of God, written in the Bible, has had its day anyway. All poetry in all languages will no longer be understood either. This artificial language will be largely digital, i.e. a programme language that can be entered in any laptop at the push of a button. As thought is extensively linked to language, thought will become superfluous.

The Fourth Commandment
RULE PASSION-
FAITH TRADITION

This can be understood to mean that the government will determine by simple decree how convictions, beliefs and traditions are to be practiced.

The Fifth Commandment

PROTECT PEOPLE AND
NATIONS   WITH FAIR LAWS
AND JUST COURTS

This instruction is not credible. According to the preceding, there will be no people or nations left. Everything will be homogenised. There are also no laws according to which courts of law must judge; at least, no laws are mentioned.

The Sixth Commandment
LET ALL NATIONS RULE
INTERNALLY
RESOLVING   EXTERNAL
DISPUTES IN A WORLD
COURT

This commandment is also deceptive. There can of course be a world court. But if all nations are disbanded, how are they to solve internal difficulties themselves?

The Seventh Commandment
AVOID PETTY LAWS AND
USELESS OFFICIALS

One can surmise that petty laws mean the laws of the Decalogue:

You shall not murder

You shall not steal

You shall not commit adultery

Judges who watch over these laws would therefore be superfluous and useless. There will be no property or land ownership in these new societies. Government will allocate a basic monthly income to everyone and provide them with the housing they need. As there will be no family, there will be no adultery either. The total control over the individual no longer allows him to kill and murder anyway.

The Eighth Commandment
BALANCE PERSONAL
RIGHTS WITH SOCIAL
DUTIES

This, too, is only an empty phrase, as personal rights don't exist anymore. Social duty means following government's instructions.

The Ninth Commandment
PRIZE TRUTH BEAUTY-
LOVE-   SEEKING
HARMONY WITH THE
INFINITE

A nice final sentence that can be compared to our sentence in the Constitution: Human dignity is inviolable. Which means that the sentence is totally empty.

The Tenth Commandment

BE NOT A CANCER ON
THE EARTH — LEAVE
ROOM FOR NATURE —
LEAVE ROOM FOR
NATURE

A wonderful final sentence. Man, and humanity in its entirety is a cancerous growth on the earth. The best would be for it to take itself out so that there is room for nature. The Satanic quest to exterminate humanity is attested from the very beginning in the Old Testament. At last, the Satanists are showing their true colours.

Additional remark

What is striking, and throws light on the authors of these commandments, is that the German language and the importance of Germanness in the thousand-year history from the earliest Middle Ages to the present day is completely left out. The Holy Roman Empire of the German Nation, which has played the dominant role in culture and politics in central Europe for more than a thousand years from Charlemagne's coronation on, is completely ignored. No mention of the greatest achievements in poetry, philosophy, music and science anywhere. This is an indication that the founders of the Guidestones were guided by the hostility towards Germany that incited them into World War I and World War II. The current attempted Islamisation of Germany is a last-ditch effort to completely exterminate the German people.

Countermovement

This perceptible preparation of the Satanic forces to take over the world government does not go unnoticed, of course. The main antagonistic goal of this atheist movement is the annihilation of Christianity. At first glance, it appears to be very successful. More and more people are leaving the Church. Churches don't fill up for worship services any more. Fewer and fewer young men are willing to become priests, so that many positions in the Church remain unoccupied. Yet, outside of the Catholic and Protestant state-subsidised churches there are more and more Christians who speak of their personal conversion, and in such an individually sincere way that I have never seen before.

Christian Preachers

The usual Sunday sermon of a well-paid pastor is replaced by very personal YouTube messages from young people who zealously stand up for the faith.

Abdul Memra is a special preacher who fearlessly proclaims his convictions. He comes from Syria, from a Christian family. He grew up as Syrian Orthodox and came to the Federal Republic as a refugee. It is interesting that his mother tongue is Aramaic. This is the language that Christ himself spoke and that has survived in small parts in Syria to this day. The written language in the time of Christ was Hebrew. However, the words of the Master were handed down to us only in Greek, which was the predominant language in those day.

The Special Thing about this
Preacher

Since, as a Syrian, he also speaks the Arabic language, he can read the Quran in Arabic and his handling of issues related the Muslim faith is therefore particularly competent. He also has the ability to approach people and fellow believers directly. It was particularly impressive how he stood by Latzel when the Bremen church superiors wanted to forbid this real preacher of the words of Jesus from preaching.

Xavier Naidoo

The well-known singer has also converted to Christ and many atheists therefore find him offensive. However, Xavier is of the opinion that God the Father and the Son are different in that, in accordance with the beliefs of Jehovah's Witnesses, Christ is only a true human being, but not God. He therefore says that he does not worship Christ. This distinction between God the Father and Christ as a pure human being is an old one. The Arians professed this in the early days already. The teaching of Athanasius that Christ is true man and true God has, however, prevailed in the Catholic and Protestant Church. Abdul is convinced that Christ is also true God.

The Second Coming

The redemptive work of Christ through his death on the cross has however not been completed.

His thousand-year reign has not been established on earth yet. This goal was prepared with his resurrection. At his ascension, Christ said that the reign is being prepared and that he will come again. That, however, has been pending for two thousand years.

Imminent expectation

Christ's disciples thought that this Second Coming was going to take place in their lifetime. For centuries and two thousand years after that, the Second Coming was constantly expected but never happened. A survey among pastors in the evangelical churches has showed that only 15% of preachers themselves believed in the Second Coming. It is astonishing, however, that more and more preachers today are convinced that this Second Coming is imminent.

The End Times

If you read the Bible attentively, it becomes clear that the Second Coming will only take place in the end times. Theoretically, that could only be in thousands of years' time. But certain indications that we are living in the end times are given to us by the prophets and in Christ's Sermon on the Mount.

The Role of Israel

Israel plays a central role in these end times. It is revealed that the Jews from all over the world are returning to their land and that the third temple will be built. This really is an absolutely new development after Jews were scattered around the world for two thousand years. The revelations of the prophet Daniel and Zechariah can now be understood literally, as can Christ's Sermon on the Mount.

Swiss Preachers

Switzerland did not become as Americanised as the Federal Republic of Germany. That is why a lot of conservative thought on biblical interpretation and politics come from there. Liebi, Lieth, but also individual pastors from German Protestant churches, Gassmann, Schilling, etc. interpret the Bible surprisingly literally, which until recently was completely unthinkable.

Seven Weeks of Years

The prophet Daniel speaks of seven weeks of years. The first half is another period of grace for humanity and an opportunity for conversion and repentance. After that, there is no more salvation. It is not known exactly when the end time will start. However, many signs point to the fact that it has already started. Thorsten Schulte declared 1 August 2020, the day of the freedom of Berlin, as the start of the apocalypse. Apocalypse was translated by Luther as the Revelation of John. The meaning of the word apocalypse is literally "revelation". Schulte interprets it as that the exposure of the criminal machinations of the great governments begins on this day.

The Rapture

This word has only recently played a major role for the first time, because it is one of the strangest prophecies of all. Two people cross the field together; one is taken away in seconds and the other is left behind. The raptured one is raised into heaven straight to the side of Christ.

This rapture is a token of grace for Christians who do not have to endure the tribulation of the last three and a half years. It is almost inconceivable that hundreds of thousands of people can disappear in a flash. The astonishment of those that are left behind will not find an explanation for this.

144,000

These are the 12,000 from each tribe of Israel that will be saved. After Israel, with a few exceptions, has rejected faith in Christ, this mass conversion of 144,000 will take place in Jerusalem in the end times. This is how the preachers interpret biblical prophecies.

The Concrete, Real Situation

Christ says: "When it comes to the weather, you look at the signs that announce the weather that is coming. But you don't do that when the end times are announced." But more and more preachers today recognise these signs, and that the end times are indeed approaching. People are only now able to understand the prophecies that were revealed for this end time. They are sometimes even interpreted literally, in a way that would not have been possible at earlier times.

3 1/2 years of peace

Daniel's prophecies refer specifically to this end time, even though the prophet lived several centuries before Christ. Several experienced exponents of Bible passages are convinced that his sayings refer to the present time. They are convinced that the great catastrophe of the end times will not occur immediately, but there will be a delay of 3 ½ years for repentance and conversion. They even assume that there will be an almost paradisiacal short period of peace.

Peace Treaty

A peace treaty will herald the beginning of the end times. This could possibly be the expected peace treaty between Putin and Trump. A revision of Yalta is aimed at revising the agreed regulation of the victorious powers in 1944. Even Germany is to become sovereign again, and the occupation rights that the Americans in particular still claim for themselves will no longer apply. Even the Near East, i.e. Israel and Palestine, will be pacified. A start has been made on this.

The Destruction of Israel

According to the instructions of the prophet Daniel, calculations are made in seven weeks of years. Every week corresponds to one year. After the first half, a time of peace, the second period will start with the destruction of Israel. The last battle of Armageddon will completely destroy the secular state of Israel. This is what most Bible scholars surmise. All Muslim states will unite and take action against Israel: Turkey, Iraq, Iran, Pakistan and Indonesia. Such a slaughter will of course have repercussions for the entire world.

Transformation

"Flesh and blood", however, cannot inherit the Kingdom of God. Therefore, the human being must be "transformed".

"See, I tell you a mystery," says Paul in the first
epistle to the Corinthians 15:50-58:
"I declare to you, brothers and sisters, that flesh and blood cannot inherit the Kingdom of God, nor does the perishable inherit the imperishable.

Listen, I tell you a mystery: We will not all sleep, but we will all be changed — in a flash, in the twinkling of an eye, at the last trumpet. For the trumpet will sound, the dead will be raised imperishable, and we will be changed."

Brahms

Brahms set these words to music in his German Requiem. This is one of the most powerful musical compositions. You can listen to this composition in video on the Internet. I regard the fact that we're able to do it as a gift of grace from God that the Internet has given us.

Second Creation

"See, I have overcome the world", i.e. the old creation has come to an end. A new creation begins with Christ. The New Adam was created, as well as a new heaven and a new earth.

Inconceivable

"What no eye has seen and no ear has heard", Paul writes, that is the "Kingdom of God". We don't even want to imagine it. We are not capable of doing so, but we are looking forward to it.

Turning Point

History always takes place in caesurae and turning points. I would like to discuss two of them in more depth. They are the surprising events that led two people on whom all hope for world peace rests to step onto the world political stage.

30

May 2000

Yeltsin, the President of the Russian Federation, did not appoint his crown prince Boris Nemzov his successor, but rather Vladimir Putin, who was completely unknown at the time.

Nemzov

Nemzov was the favourite of the Wall Street finance elite. In exchange for their generous support, he had already promised them that all state-owned companies would be privatised so that for people for whom money is no issue, all deposits of mineral resources in the giant realm could be bought cheaply and exploited by their US companies for their personal enrichment. In addition, the state-run press would go into private ownership, with the result being that a press mogul could buy up all the newspapers and, as with our mainstream media, the state-sanctioned opinion of the West would be the only one to be spread in Russia.

NZZ

The Neue Zürcher Zeitung was the only independent newspaper in the German-speaking world for many years. In the meantime, this newspaper has also had to print the standard articles from dpa and Reuters because for financial reasons it no longer has the option of letting its own journalists do research.

20/01/2017

This date marks the point in time when Trump delivered his inauguration speech as US President against all odds and any prognosis. Even his election victory borders on being a miracle. The establishment supported the rival candidate, Hillary Clinton, with 1 billion dollars, and the press — New York Times, Washington Post, TV, CNN, BBC, etc. fought exclusively for Hillary to be elected and collected everything negative that could be found about Trump over decades.

Planned Assassination

When all that did not work, an assassination attempt was planned. He was to be taken out immediately before starting his speech; namely at the point where his private protection team was replaced by the official presidential guard.

Model

This assassination was to be based on the model with which F.D. Roosevelt had his competitor removed in order to ensure that he'd win the election in 1932. A high-ranking and influential person, whose name of course remains anonymous, is said to have revealed this plan to Trump. It could possibly be the anonymous one = Anon. Possibly the same person who appears in the Signum Qanon.

Expectation

The rumour of such an assassination attempt can of course not be confirmed. There are, however, indications that the rumour contains some truth. Had the attack succeeded, Obama would have been able to continue running the government. That was the officially expressed wish. But when it didn't succeed, attempts were immediately made at all levels to remove Trump from his office, right up to the violent "He's not my president" street battles financed by Soros.

We are familiar with such scenes in countries where election results are not recognised as a matter of principle. The phenomenon is new to the USA, as surely the purpose of elections is that the will of the majority should be accepted.

Amazement of the guests
of honour

The guests of honour, all the former presidents of the USA who were still alive, were astonished when Trump, after a certain delay, appeared for the inauguration with First Lady Melania and gave his first address as President to the American people. They clearly hadn't reckoned with that.

Jimmy Carter

He was the oldest among them. He is now older than 90. He is the only one with Christian roots. He is a Baptist. He tried without success to instil moral values in the politics of his time. However, in the USA, policy is not decided by the President, but rather by the CIA, and is secret. Presidents are only initiated in the secret operations if they play the game. In government, too, only a few members are informed. The majority of the representatives in the Senate and Congress are completely clueless about what is going on in secret.

Death threats

As Carter refused to play their game, the CIA informed him with brutal honesty that if he didn't toe the line, they would do to him what they did to John F. Kennedy. It is obvious that Kennedy was murdered by the "Deep State" because he wanted to nationalise the private bank FED. It was also clear that Carter was not going to be allowed to take up a second term.

Bush Junior

He is responsible for the disastrous war in Iraq. After he had determined that Saddam Hussein did not possess weapons of mass destruction, meaning that it was safe for Americans to go to war, he justified his attack with the infamous demand that if Saddam did not voluntarily produce his weapons of mass destruction, an attack would be inevitable. As Saddam could not do this even if he wanted to, as he actually did not have any, war was inevitable for Bush.

Consequences

Such a declaration of war is so unique that it made all those who advocate for truthfulness in politics rethink. From that point on, it became clear that the US government does not stand for human rights and the well-being of the nations, but that it is the number one rogue state in the world.

Richard Clinton

The CIA set Monica Lewinsky on him. The intention was to blackmail him through a sexual affair to abolish the "bank separation system".

There are savings banks, and then there are investment banks. At a savings bank, the saver can invest his money at a low interest rate and the bank can then lend this money out at a higher interest rate. The difference in interest is the profit the bank makes. However, the bank may only lend this money of its savers against collateral, pledge or mortgage. In this way, it is unlikely that the bank won't be able to repay the money it's taken from savings to lend out again, and losing all your money is almost impossible. In other words: savings banks have little opportunity to embezzle their clients' money.

Investment Banks

It is a different matter at investment banks. They advise customers on how and where to invest their money. They can even invest customers' cash themselves. Preferably, of course, where they get the highest commission, which means in bonds and securities, which have no value in themselves and can only be sold because of the high commissions and bonus payments. If the bank separation system is abolished, savings banks may also invest their customers' money in worthless pieces of paper as they see fit. Then a bank can file for bankruptcy, and thus legally deprive its customers of their wealth.

Hillary Clinton

She also sat in the first line of guests of honour, together with her husband. It was a given that she should have become President instead of Trump. The billionaires of Wall Street, the arms industry, the entire press, TV, radio, Hollywood stars, etc. they all supported her. Even before she became president, hundreds of millions were thrown at her in the expectation that the war against Iran that was promised to Israel would take place. Indeed, a nuclear war limited to Europe would bring the hated Putin to his knees. A case of the general population suffering in their millions, but where the elite smelt a brilliant profitable transaction.

Obama

And among those seated was Obama as well, and his Michelle who is so adored by the press. A mass murderer who was awarded the Nobel Peace Prize at the beginning of his term in office to hide the fact that he was waging war in six countries at the same time. He also started the most hideous of modern warfare: drone warfare, in Yemen.

This is done like a digital game. The "perpetrator" sits in safety, thousands of kilometres from the place of action, in his office in Ramstein. He steers the remotely but automatically controlled bomb-laden drone into a crowd that he sees on his television screen, because a crowd could mean a riot, especially because an individual among them may have been recognised by remote detection and could possibly belong to a terrorist organisation. If civilians who are totally uninvolved are among the crowd, they are labelled collateral damage. In this way, Obama had an average of ten people a day killed for years. Angela Merkel was content and happy with him
as the "best friend" at the Protestant church convention.

Reaction of the Guests

These are the guests, the guests of honour in the first row, before whom Trump gives his speech. You can imagine their faces when Trump speaks about the quagmire in Washington D.C. The camera team dared to capture and broadcast only a few moments of this. But the criminals present there couldn't hide their reaction at thereby being exposed in public.

Drum Roll

The first sentence of Trump's inauguration speech is a bang that those addressed will have understood immediately: He promises to rebuild the country — to rebuild the nation — which these presidents, as the last in a line of many miserable presidents, drove into the ground. And he renews the promises made to the people when the USA was founded in 1776 and which the successive governments had broken long ago, namely "government by the people, for the people".

Reality

The government of the USA has absolutely no relation to the people.

The wars conducted all over the world were exclusively in the interest of the financial elite and large corporations. The government representatives are only puppets of this "establishment". In a few cases even central members of the seven most influential families in the United States, e.g. both the Roosevelts, Theodor and Franklin Delano.

How many understood that?

Except for the four presidents, the guests of honour in the first row, not many would have understood what Trump meant when he spoke of

"rebuilding the nation"

and

"restoring the promise".

The majority of the audience thought these two statements meant making improvements for the nation and restoring a few promises that had been neglected.

The Initiated

Only a few initiates knew that the USA hasn't existed as a nation for a long time. For many decades, policy was not conducted for the sake of the nation. Not a single project. But rather, everything was done for the profit of the banks, large corporations and oligarchs. Not one enterprise was aimed at the well-being of the people. The notion at the founding of the nation, "government by the people, for the people", was completely forgotten.

A Small Group

Then Trumps directs himself to the presidents present: a small group that had sat and governed in the capital Washington D.C. To them he says that they had "reaped the rewards of government" while the people had borne the costs.

Embarrassing

Now at last it becomes apparent to those who are last in line; embarrassing for those physically present, before the eyes of the American nation and seen millions of times on television: the exposure of the rulers, visible to the whole world, who gathered their riches and assets at the expense of the people.

The Consequences for the People

There was nothing left of the wealth for the people. Many have lost their jobs. Factories were closed while they held lavish parties in Washington D.C. The Establishment helped themselves. Imagine these four presidents having to listen to this, especially Hillary Clinton, who is known to have snatched millions for her foundation.

About the Speech

It must be added here that Trump's speech in itself is so astonishing that it is all too easy to overlook this detail. In keeping with tradition, he starts exactly according to format. First Chief Justice Roberts is addressed, then the four last still living presidents; but then comes "fellow Americans", i.e. he calls all the others left over "fellows", meaning companions, mates. And then, quite astoundingly: "people of the world". The speech is thus directed to all people, or all the peoples of the whole world. With that, Trump wants to express that what is happening here and now, is that the United States, the most powerful country on earth, which has fallen into the hands of robbers, is to be restored as a state.

Challenge

Trump is clear about the fact that this battle will not be easy: "We will face challenge[s]." "We will confront hardships." But, he is sure: "But we will get the job done." With the difference that he will really get it done, in contrast to Germany, where the integration of asylum seekers has not been a success.

Concentrated Content

The concentrated content is not immediately clear to see. Most people would have seen the usual well-meaning declarations of intent. Such a speech simply rushes by in a matter of minutes. One can only study it attentively and in detail when it's printed.

Reaction Abroad

A non-American would have to master American English as well to be able to understand the content effortlessly. The live broadcast of the speech is also often staggered, so that not everyone is able to follow it. Apart from that, as far as Germany is concerned, not a single newspaper bothered to print the full content of the speech, let alone provide a full translation. It was the same in all Western countries: the mainstream press hushed up the speech. It was too provocative.

Replacement Spectacle

But they had to write about the official inauguration one way or another. As they couldn't possibly say anything about the content of the speech, they offered something else instead. The aim was to show that no one in the United States was interested in this inauguration and that the place in front of the Capitol was nearly empty. They showed images from Obama's inauguration: crowds of people, and empty seats for Trump. Since Trump immediately complained about this fraud, the initial reaction was "Yes, because of the rain the pictures would have been blurred at 12 o'clock, so they were replaced with pictures from 10 o'clock when the first participants arrived."

Lies

This first statement would have provided an explanation for this difference, but further broadcasts maintained that significantly fewer people were interested in Trump's inauguration than Obama's. Trump's statement was established to be a lie, and a new term was born: "alternative facts".

With that, they mean that it's not the facts that count, but rather that television determines what is recognised as facts.

Singularity

There has never been an inauguration like that of Trump, or a speech in which predecessors are unmasked to such an extent. Just because of this, the speech will enter into the annals of history.

What happens now?

It is not surprising that those addressed and the entire apparatus behind them resisted. That's why it was clear right from the start that this president could not be tolerated and had to be toppled. One impeachment process after the other. One man stands against a world of powerful people — the seven richest families in the world, who own more than half of all the money on the entire globe — and willing recipients in over a hundred countries who are bribed by these secret rulers. The only countries that oppose the "deep state" are North Korea, Iran, China and Russia.

Resistance

All the assassination attempts and impeachment processes against Trump have failed. Even in Germany, people are slowly beginning to resist the "deep state".

Corona Pandemics

In this situation, in which German citizens also rebel against the situation created by the deep state that provides for globalisation of the whole world, the corona crisis arrives, to

40

the benefit of banks and corporations. They aim to prevent a citizens' revolt through regulations such as wearing a face mask, maintaining distances and limiting mass events. The lockdown of the trade sector has engulfed it with gigantic debts that are doubling the burden of debt that businesses will not be able to repay. The aim is to destroy the middle class and production facilities in Germany, so that all that's left are the basic income recipients who are dependent on the state, as they can be manipulated through not having any rights.

Ideals

The ideals of our politics, the EU in Strasbourg and Brussels will finally be realised. This applies exactly the same for all other countries, for France, Italy, Spain, etc.

Question Marks

But maybe everything won't actually go according to Merkel's plan. There was 1 August in Berlin, and this will continue on 29 August. Maybe something can be brought about through these demonstrations. There is also reason to hope that Trump and Putin will put a stop to the goings-on in Merkel's government, which has gone mad.

Deferral

According to the interpretation of knowledgeable interpreters of the Bible, "in the fight of the devil with God" there is still a delay — a 3 ½ year period of peace — in which God gives everyone the opportunity to see how beautiful and how peaceful people could make the earth. Under the leadership of the progressive population, not only will one's own wealthy country be developed, but all other countries will benefit from it.

USA

Starting out from the USA, Central and South America will also be able to develop their incredible resources. The United States will not exploit these countries for their own purposes as colonists, but will help them as friendly nations in a win-win situation to develop their less mature infrastructures.

Russia

If the Russians invite the Germans to develop the production of their industry, an immense field of work opens up for both peoples and a monstrous prosperity can be achieved in which all peoples of Europe can participate. Heavenly conditions could prevail. The whole of Africa can be included.

China

This culture has always known how to operate on a high level, except for the three centuries of subjugation by the British Empire and the US Empire. With the Silk Road, which is to go from Shanghai to Rotterdam, the "heartland" of Eurasia will be opened up and become the most powerful centre in the world.

The Great Tribulation

However, in the opinion of almost all preachers, this situation will not last. The time of tribulation must arrive. God's judgment cannot be stopped.

Anticipation

This end-time prophecy, rather than causing fear and horror in the just, should result in joyous anticipation for Christians, as now, finally, the wish of the Lord's Prayer will be fulfilled: "Your Kingdom come". The Second Coming of Christ will finally bring about the millennial kingdom, the "Kingdom of God", in the world.

The Last Words of the Bible

"Yes, I am coming soon." These are the last words in the Revelation of John. "Amen. Come, Lord Jesus!" That is the response of the believers.